Theodore Roosevelt

Essays on Practical Politics

-

Theodore Roosevelt

Essays on Practical Politics

ISBN/EAN: 9783337068547

Printed in Europe, USA, Canada, Australia, Japan

Cover: Foto ©Suzi / pixelio.de

More available books at **www.hansebooks.com**

QUESTIONS OF THE DAY. No. XLIX.

ESSAYS

ON

PRACTICAL POLITICS

BY

THEODORE ROOSEVELT

AUTHOR OF " NAVAL WAR OF 1812-14 "

.

NEW YORK & LONDON

G. P. PUTNAM'S SONS

The Knickerbocker Press

1888

INTRODUCTION.

THESE two essays appeared originally in the *Century*. Both alike were criticised at the time as offering no cure for the evils they portrayed.

Such a criticism shows, in the first place, a curious ignorance of what is meant by the diagnosis of a disease; for my articles pretended to do nothing more than give what has apparently never before been given, an accurate account of certain phases of our political life, with its good and bad impartially set forth. The practical politician, who alone knows how our politics are really managed, is rarely willing to write about them, unless with very large reservations, while the student-reformer whose political experience is limited to the dinner table, the debating club, or an occasional mass-meeting where none but his friends are present, and who yet seeks, in pamphlet or editorial column to make clear the subject, hardly ever knows exactly what he is talking about, and abuses the system in all its parts with such looseness of language as to wholly take away the value even from such of his utterances as are true.

In the second place, such a criticism shows in the mind of the critic the tendency, so common among imperfectly educated people, to clamor for "cure-all" or quack remedies. The same habit of thought that makes a man in one class of life demand a medicine that will ease all his complaints off-hand, makes another man, who probably considers himself very much higher in the social scale, expect some scheme of reform that will at a single fell swoop do away with every evil from which the body-politic is suffering. Each of these men is willing enough to laugh at the other ; and, after all, their inconsistency is no greater than is that of the editor who in one column denounces governmental interference with the hours of labor, and in the next calls for governmental interference with the party primaries, or *vice versa*, apparently not seeing that both are identical in kind, being perhaps necessary deviations from the old American principle that the State must not interfere with individual action, even to help the weak.

There are many reforms each of which, if accomplished, would do us much good; but for permanent improvement we must rely upon bettering our general health, upon raising the tone of our political system. Thus, the enactment and enforcement of laws making the Merit System, as contrasted with the Spoils System, universally applicable among all minor officials of county, state and nation, would measurably improve our public service and would be of immeasurable benefit to all honest men, rich or poor, who desire to do their duty in public affairs without being opposed to bands of trained mercenaries. The regulation of the liquor traffic, so as to expose it to strict supervision, and to minimize its attendant evils, would likewise do immense good. But even if the power of the saloons was broken and public office no longer a reward for partisan service, many and great evils would remain to be battled with.

No law or laws can give us good government; at the utmost, they can only give us the opportunity to ourselves get good government. For instance, until the control of the aldermen over the mayor's appointments was taken away, by the bill which I always esteemed it my chief legislative service to have introduced and been instrumental in passing, New York city politics were hopeless; now it rests with the citizens themselves to elect a man who will serve them wisely and faithfully.

But no law can make an ignorant workman cease to pay heed to the demagogue who bids for his vote by proposing impossible measures of relief; no law can make a rich young man go to his party primary even if it comes on the same night as a club dinner or a german at Delmonico's. There are few things more harmful or more irritating than the insolence with which some classes of immigrants persist in dragging in to our own affairs questions of purely foreign politics, with which we should have nothing to do; even more despicable is the attitude of truckling servility toward these same foreigners on the part of native-born citizens who seem content to run an American congressional contest as if it were an election for the British parliament, with such issues as Home Rule and the Land League on one side, and the preservation of the union between England and Ireland on the other. But it is difficult to see how we can remedy all this by legislation. We must rouse public sentiment against it, and make people understand that while we welcome all honest immigrants who come prepared to cast in their lot with us, and live under our institutions, and while we treat them in every respect as

standing on the same level with ourselves, we demand
in return that they shall drop all connections with foreign politics, shall teach their children to "talk United
States," and shall learn to celebrate the Fourth of July
instead of St. Patrick's Day, and the birthday of Washington instead of that of either Queen or Kaiser.

We can do a good deal of good by passing new, or
extending the scope of old, laws. We can begin the
work of keeping out undesirable immigrants, and we
cannot possibly begin it too soon. We can totally abol-
ish the now wholly useless or harmful board of aldermen. We can provide for a reform in the method of preparing and distributing ballots (perhaps the matter which
is at present of most pressing importance), and for putting
the Merit System on a firmer and broader basis. We
can attempt to diminish by the introduction of high
license, and otherwise, the evils attendant upon the liquor
or traffic. We can pass severe laws against bribery and
strive to have them executed (as the City Reform Club has
recently striven). We can prevent all hostile interference
with our public school system. We can if necessary
strengthen the provisions of the Common Law so as to
insure the prompt punishment of those communists and
dynamite agitators who attempt to put their theories
into practise or incite others to do so. But much more
remains. We must try to reward good, and punish bad,
public servants. We can hardly do too much honor to
the court and jury that condemned, or to the governor
who refused to pardon, the Chicago anarchists and
bomb-throwers; or to the judge who distributed stern
and even justice to the boycotters on the one hand, and

on the other to the bribed aldermen and the wealthy knave who bribed them. Those of us who are newspaper writers can refrain from scurrilous abuse of political opponents; and from the incessant innuendo which is quite as harmful and even meaner. Above all, we can strive to fulfil our own political duties, as they arise, and thereby to do each of us his part in raising to a healthier level the moral standard of the whole community.

In conclusion, let me quote the words of a man who, while a private citizen has yet been always, in the highest sense of the word, a public servant; I quote from a speech recently made by Joseph Choate (the italics are my own):—

" I confidently believe that the decay of our politics which all must acknowledge has arisen in no small measure from the neglect of their political rights and duties, for the last twenty years, by the great body of the educated men of the country, and the still greater body of the business men of the country, whereby the management of party affairs has been left so largely to those who make it a trade and a profession; and so I hail with delight and satisfaction the revival of interest and action in any form, in these great representative classes of the community.

" The renewed attention which has been given of late years in all our leading colleges and universities to the study of political economy and other public and constitutional studies, is one of the most cheering signs of the times; and if by this or any other means the great body of our young graduates as they enter into active life can

be inspired with the earnest purpose to be faithful to
their political duties and trusts, the much needed reform
will be already secured. The truth is that, in all our
great cities especially, the struggle for professional and
business success is so intense, the struggle for existence
and position so overwhelming, that the plea is too often
accepted that our best men have no time for consideration and action upon public affairs. But if our institutions and liberties are worth saving, they can only be
saved by eternal vigilance and action on the part of those
whose education and interest in the public welfare
qualify them to take part in the public questions on
which it depends. Our unexampled material progress
and success are in one respect our greatest danger; but
the true antidote to the intense and growing materialism
of the age and country is in the hands of our educated
men, and if these fail us, we may well despair. ' There
is surely no lack among us of the raw material of states-
manship,' * * * * * and when any great peril
overhangs the country, as in the case of our Civil War,
great men will be ready for the emergency, and new Lin-
colns and Stantons and Grants will arise to meet it. *But
what I plead for is a little more—yes, a great deal more—
of attention in ordinary times to public duties, on the part
of those who are qualified to discharge them; and so, and
so only, shall we have purer politics and better government.*"

THEODORE ROOSEVELT.

ESSAYS ON

PRACTICAL POLITICS.

PHASES OF STATE LEGISLATION.

THE ALBANY LEGISLATURE.

FEW persons realize the magnitude of the interests affected by State legislation in New York. It is no mere figure of speech to call New York the Empire State; and most of the laws directly and immediately affecting the interests of its citizens are passed at Albany, and not at Washington. In fact, there is at Albany a little Home Rule Parliament which presides over the destinies of a commonwealth more populous than any one of two-thirds of the kingdoms of Europe, and one which, in point of wealth, material prosperity, variety of interests, extent of territory, and capacity for expansion, can fairly be said to rank next to the powers of the first class. This little parliament, composed of one hundred and twenty-eight members in the Assembly and thirty-two in the Senate, is, in the fullest sense of the term, a *representative* body; there is hardly one of the many and widely diversified interests of the State that has not a mouth-piece at Albany, and hardly a single class of its citizens—not even excepting, I regret to say, the criminal class—which lacks its representative among the legis-

7

lators. In the three Legislatures of which I have been
a member, I have sat with bankers and bricklayers, with
merchants and mechanics, with lawyers, farmers, day-
laborers, saloon-keepers, clergymen, and prize-fighters.
Among my colleagues there were many very good men;
there was a still more numerous class of men who were
neither very good nor very bad, but went one way or the
other, according to the strength of the various conflict-
ing influences acting around, behind, and upon them;
and, finally there were many very bad men. Still, the
New York Legislature, taken as a whole, is by no means
as bad a body as we would be led to believe if our judgment was based purely on what we read in the great
metropolitan papers; for the custom of the latter is to
portray things as either very much better or very much
worse than they are.* Where a number of men, many
of them poor, some of them unscrupulous, and others
elected by constituents too ignorant to hold them to a
proper accountability for their actions, are put into a
position of great temporary power, where they are called
to take action upon questions affecting the welfare of

---

* As a piece of refreshingly wholesome common-sense let me give the
following extract from a recent speech of Mr. Edward Everett Hale; it is
especially good reading for the young man who has been educated in the
belief that it is a sign of cultivation and refinement to sneer at those who
take an active part in American politics, and for the newspaper writer who
annually refers to every New York Legislature, good or bad, as "the worst
since the days of Tweed."

" I do not think, indeed, that the critics, on this side or on the other side,
rightly comprehend the value of the services which loyal men render in
State Legislatures in the government of this country. They do not comprehend the importance of the trust committed to those men. It is a great
thing to be the representative, for all the purposes of legislation of the

large corporations and wealthy private individuals, the chances for corruption are always great, and that there is much viciousness and political dishonesty, much moral cowardice, and a good deal of actual bribe-taking in Albany, no one who has had any practical experience of legislation can doubt; but, at the same time, I think that the good members always outnumber the bad, and that there is never any doubt as to the result when a naked question of right or wrong can be placed clearly and in its true light before the Legislature. The trouble is that on many questions the Legislature never does have the right and wrong clearly shown it. Either some bold, clever parliamentary tactician snaps the measure through before the members are aware of its nature, or else the obnoxious features are so combined with good ones as to procure the support of a certain proportion of that large class of men whose intentions are excellent but whose intellects are foggy.

State of New York, of forty or fifty thousand persons. I will not pretend to give accurate figures, but on a rough estimate, I suppose that every member of the lower house at Albany represents about forty-three thousand people. I understand that, on the recent estimates in England, every Member of Parliament represents forty-six or forty-seven thousand people on the average. The contrast, then, when you are speaking of public service, should be, not simply between the number of educated men in the State of New York who go into Congress, and the number of educated men who go into the British Parliament. It should fairly take into account the number of men who go into your State Legislature.

"* * * * * I doubt very much if the current habit, either of the press or of private conversation, does justice to the loyal work which is done by the members of the State Legislatures of this country—a work to which this country is very largely indebted. If I, an outsider, may be permitted to speak of the Legislature in Albany, * * * * * at this mo-

THE CHARACTER OF THE REPRESENTATIVES.

THE representatives from different sections of the
State differ widely in character.   Those from the country
districts are generally very good men.   They are usually
well-to-do farmers, small lawyers, or prosperous store-
keepers, and are shrewd, quiet, and honest.   They are
often narrow-minded and slow to receive an idea ; but,
on the other hand, when they get a good one, they cling
to it with the utmost tenacity.   They form very much
the most valuable class of legislators.   For the most
part they are native Americans, and those who are not
are men who have become completely Americanized
in all their ways and habits of thought.   One of the most
useful members of the last Legislature was a German
from a western county, and the extent of his Ameri-
canization can be judged from the fact that he was
actually an ardent prohibitionist : certainly no one who
knows Teutonic human nature will require further proof.
Again, I sat for an entire session beside a very intelligent
member from northern New York before I discovered

---

ment I remember three gentlemen whom I have known, and but three gentlemen whom I have known, who were members of that body.   I should be
sorry not to say that those three gentlemen would have done honor to any
legislative body of which I ever read, since legislative bodies have taken on
the form which they have assumed in modern times.[1]   Wherever gentlemen
go, I beg they will remember that the duty which they do in politics, as
members of the local government of their cities, or of the state government
of their States, is to be compared, not unfavorably, with the work which is
done by the few men who, under our system, can be Members of Congress.

[(1) I have been privately asked who were the persons to whom I alluded.
There is no reason why I should not name them.   One was the late Vice-
President of the United States, Mr. Wheeler ; one was the Honorable Carl-
ton Sprague of Buffalo ; one was the Honorable Andrew White of Ithaca.]

that he was an Irishman; all his views of legislation, even upon such subjects as free schools and the impropriety of making appropriations from the treasury for the support of sectarian institutions, were precisely similar to those of his Protestant American neighbors, though he was himself a Catholic. Now a German or an Irishman from one of the great cities would have retained most of his national peculiarities.

It is from these same great cities that the worst legislators come. It is true that there are always among them a few cultivated and scholarly men who are well educated, and who stand on a higher and broader intellectual and moral plane than the country members, but the bulk are very low indeed. They are usually foreigners, of little or no education, with exceedingly misty ideas as to morality, and possessed of an ignorance so profound that it could only be called comic, were it not for the fact that it has at times such serious effects upon our laws. It is their ignorance, quite as much as actual viciousness, which makes it so difficult to procure the passage of good laws or prevent the passage of bad ones; and it is the most irritating of the many elements with which we have to contend in the fight for good government.

DARK SIDE OF THE LEGISLATIVE PICTURE.

MENTION has been made above of the bribe-taking which undoubtedly at times occurs in the New York Legislature. This is what is commonly called "a delicate subject" with which to deal, and, therefore, according to our usual methods of handling delicate subjects, it is either never discussed at all, or else discussed with the grossest exaggeration; but most certainly there is nothing about which it is more important to know the truth.

In each of the last three Legislatures* there were a number of us who were interested in getting through certain measures which we deemed to be for the public good, but which were certain to be strongly opposed, some for political and some for pecuniary reasons. Now, to get through any such measure requires genuine hard work, a certain amount of parliamentary skill, a good deal of tact and courage, and, above all, a thorough knowledge of the men with whom one has to deal, and of the motives which actuate them. In other words, before taking any active steps, we had to "size up" our fellow legislators, to find out their past history and present character and associates, to find out whether they were their own masters or were acting under the directions of somebody else, whether they were bright or stupid, etc., etc. As a result, and after very careful study, conducted purely with the object of learning the truth, so that we might work more effectually, we came to the conclusion that about a third of the members were open to corrupt influences in some form or other; in certain sessions the proportion was greater, and in some less. Now it would, of course, be impossible for me or for anyone else to prove in a court of law that these men were guilty, except perhaps in two or three cases; yet we felt absolutely confident that there was hardly a case in which our judgment as to the

* Written in January, 1885.

honesty of any given member was not correct. The two or three exceptional cases alluded to, where legal proof of guilt might have been forthcoming, were instances in which honest men were approached by their colleagues at times when the need for votes was very great; but, even then, it would have been almost impossible to punish the offenders before a court, for it would have merely resulted in his denying what his accuser stated. Moreover, the members who had been approached would have been very reluctant to come forward, for each of them felt ashamed that his character should not have been well enough known to prevent anyone's daring to speak to him on such a subject. And another reason why the few honest men who are approached (for the lobbyist rarely makes a mistake in his estimate of the men who will be apt to take bribes) do not feel like taking action in the matter is that a doubtful lawsuit will certainly follow, which will drag on so long that the public will come to regard all of the participants with equal distrust, while in the end the decision is quite as likely to be against as to be for them. Take the Bradly-Sessions case, for example. This was an incident that occurred at the time of the faction-fight in the Republican ranks over the return of Mr. Conkling to the Senate after his resignation from that body. Bradly, an assemblyman, accused Sessions, a State senator, of attempting to bribe him. The affair dragged on for an indefinite time; no one was able actually to determine whether it was a case of blackmail on the one hand, or of bribery on the other; the vast majority of people recollected the names of both parties, but totally forgot.

which it was that was supposed to have bribed the other, and regarded both with equal disfavor; and the upshot has been that the case is now merely remembered as illustrating one of the most unsavory phases of the famous Half-breed-Stalwart fight.

DIFFICULTIES OF PREVENTING AND PUNISHING CORRUPTION.

FROM the causes indicated, it is almost impossible to actually convict a legislator of bribe-taking; but at the same time, the character of a legislator, if bad, soon becomes a matter of common notoriety, and no dishonest legislator can long keep his reputation good with honest men. If the constituents wish to know the character of their member, they can easily find it out, and no member will be dishonest if he thinks his constituents are looking at him; he presumes upon their ignorance or indifference. I do not see how bribe-taking among legislators can be stopped until the public conscience, which is, even now, gradually awakening, becomes *fully* awake to the matter. Then it will stop fast enough; for just as soon as politicians realize that the people are in earnest in wanting a thing done, they make haste to do it. The trouble is always in rousing the people sufficiently to make them take an *effective* interest,—that is, in making them sufficiently in earnest to be willing to give a little of their time to the accomplishment of the object they have in view.

Much the largest percentage of corrupt legislators come from the great cities; indeed, the majority of the assemblymen from the great cities are " very poor specimens" indeed, while, on the contrary, the congressmen who go from them are generally pretty good men. This fact is only one of the many which go to establish the curious political law that in a great city the larger the constituency which elects a public servant, the more apt that servant is to be a good one; exactly as the mayor is almost certain to be infinitely superior in character to the average alderman, or the average city judge to the average civil justice. This is because the public servants of comparatively small importance are protected by their own insignificance from the consequences of their bad actions. Life is carried on at such a high pressure in the great cities, men's time is so fully occupied by their manifold and harassing interests and duties, and their knowledge of their neighbors is necessarily so limited, that they are only able to fix in their minds the characters and records of a few prominent men; the others they lump together without distinguishing between individuals. They know whether the aldermen, as a body, are to be admired or despised; but they probably do not even know the name, far less the worth, of the particular alderman who represents their district; so it happens that their votes for aldermen or assemblymen are generally given with very little intelligence indeed, while, on the contrary, they are fully competent to pass and execute judgment upon as prominent an official as a mayor or even a congressman. Hence it follows that the latter have to give a good deal of attention to the wishes and prejudices of the public at large, while a city assemblyman, though he always talks a great deal about the people, rarely, except in certain extraordinary cases, has

to pay much heed to their wants. His political future
depends far more upon the skill and success with which
he cultivates the good-will of certain "bosses," or of
certain cliques of politicians, or even of certain bodies
and knots of men (such as compose a trade-union, or a
collection of merchants in some special business, or the
managers of a railroad) whose interests, being vitally
affected by Albany legislation, oblige them closely to
watch, and to try to punish or reward, the Albany legislators. These politicians or sets of interested individuals
generally care very little for a man's honesty so long as
he can be depended upon to do as they wish on certain
occasions ; and hence it often happens that a dishonest
man who has sense enough not to excite attention by
any flagrant outrage may continue for a number of years
to represent an honest constituency.

THE CONSTITUENTS LARGELY TO BLAME.

MOREOVER, a member from a large city can often
count upon the educated and intelligent men of his district showing the most gross ignorance and stupidity in
political affairs. The much-lauded intelligent voter—the
man of cultured mind, liberal education, and excellent
intentions—at times performs exceedingly queer antics.

The great public meetings to advance certain political
movements irrespective of party, which have been held
so frequently during the past few years, have undoubtedly done a vast amount of good; but the very men
who attend these public meetings and inveigh against
the folly and wickedness of the politicians will sometimes
on election day do things which have quite as evil effects

as any of the acts of the men whom they very properly condemn. A recent instance of this is worth giving. In 1882 there was in the Assembly a young member from New York, who did as hard and effective work for the city of New York as has ever been done by anyone. It was a peculiarly disagreeable year to be in the Legislature. The composition of that body was unusually bad. The more disreputable politicians relied upon it to pass some of their schemes and to protect certain of their members from the consequences of their own misdeeds. Demagogic measures were continually brought forward, nominally in the interests of the laboring classes, for which an honest and intelligent man could not vote, and yet which were jealously watched by, and received the hearty support of, not only mere demagogues and agitators, but also a large number of perfectly honest though misguided working men. And, finally, certain wealthy corporations attempted, by the most unscrupulous means, to rush through a number of laws in their own interest. The young member of whom we are speaking incurred by his course on these various measures the bitter hostility alike of the politicians, the demagogues, and the members of that most dangerous of all classes, the wealthy criminal class. He had also earned the gratitude of all honest citizens, and he got it—as far as words went. The better class of newspapers spoke well of him; cultured and intelligent men generally—the well-to-do, prosperous people who belong to the different social and literary clubs, and their followers—were loud in his praise. I call to mind one man who lived in his district who expressed great indignation that the politi-

2

cians should dare to oppose his reëlection ; when told that
it was to be hoped he would help to insure the legislator's return to Albany by himself staying at the polls all
day, he answered that he was very sorry, but he unfortunately had an engagement to go quail-shooting on
election-day! Most respectable people, however, would
undoubtedly have voted for and reëlected the young
member had it not been for the unexpected political
movements that took place in the fall. A citizens'
ticket, largely non-partisan in character, was run for
certain local offices, receiving its support from among
those who claimed to be, and who undoubtedly were,
the best men of both parties. The ticket contained the
names of candidates only for municipal offices, and
had nothing whatever to do with the election of men to
the Legislature ; yet it proved absolutely impossible to
drill this simple fact through the heads of a great many
worthy people, who, when election-day came round, de-
clined to vote anything but the citizens' ticket, and per-
sisted in thinking that if no legislative candidate was on
the ticket, it was because, for some reason or other, the
citizens' committee did not consider any legislative candidate worth voting for. All over the city the better
class of candidates for legislative offices lost from this
cause votes which they had a right to expect, and in the
particular district under consideration the loss was so
great as to cause the defeat of the sitting member, or
rather to elect him by so narrow a vote as to enable an
unscrupulously partisan legislative majority to keep him
out of his seat.

It is this kind of ignorance of the simplest political

matters among really good citizens, combined with their timidity, which is so apt to characterize a wealthy *bourgeoisie*, and with their short-sighted selfishness in being unwilling to take the smallest portion of time away from their business or pleasure to devote to public affairs, which renders it so easy for corrupt men from the city to keep their places in the Legislature. In the country the case is different. Here the constituencies, who are usually composed of honest though narrow-minded and bigoted individuals, generally keep a pretty sharp look-out on their members, and, as already said, the latter are apt to be fairly honest men. Even when they are not honest, they take good care to act perfectly well as regards all district matters, for most of the measures about which corrupt influences are at work relate to city affairs. The constituents of a country member know well how to judge him for those of his acts which immediately affect themselves; but, as regards others, they often have no means of forming an opinion, except through the newspapers,—more especially through the great metropolitan newspapers,—and they have gradually come to look upon all statements made by the latter with reference to the honesty or dishonesty of public men with extreme distrust. This is because the newspapers, including those who professedly stand as representatives of the highest culture of the community, have been in the habit of making such constant and reckless assaults upon the characters of even very good public men, as to greatly detract from their influence when they attack one who is really bad. They paint every one with whom they disagree black. As a consequence the average man,

who knows they are partly wrong, thinks they may also
be partly right ; he concludes that no man is absolutely
white, and at the same time that no one is as black as he
is painted; and takes refuge in the belief that all alike
are gray. It then becomes impossible to rouse him to
make an effort either for a good man or against a scoun-
drel. Nothing helps dishonest politicians as much as
this feeling; and among the chief instruments in its pro-
duction we must number certain of our newspapers who
are loudest in asserting that they stand on the highest
moral plane.

PERILS OF LEGISLATIVE LIFE.

However, there can be no question that a great many
men do deteriorate very much morally when they go to
Albany. The last accusation most of us would think of
bringing against that dear, dull, old Dutch city is that of
being a fast place ; and yet there are plenty of members
coming from out-of-the-way villages or quiet country
towns on whom Albany has as bad an effect as Paris
sometimes has on wealthy young Americans from the
great seaboard cities. Many men go to the Legislature
with the set purpose of making money ; but many
others, who afterwards become bad, go there intending
to do good work. These latter may be well-meaning,
weak young fellows of some shallow brightness, who expect to make names for themselves ; perhaps they are
young lawyers, or real-estate brokers, or small shopkeep-
ers ; they achieve but little success ; they gradually become conscious that their business is broken up, and that
they have not enough ability to warrant any expectation

of their continuing in public life; some great temptation comes in their way (a corporation which expects to be relieved of perhaps a million dollars of taxes by the passage of a bill can afford to pay high for voters); they fall, and that is the end of them. Indeed, legislative life has temptations enough to make it unadvisable for any weak man, whether young or old, to enter it.

ALLIES OF VICIOUS LEGISLATORS.

THE array of vicious legislators is swelled by a number of men who really at bottom are not bad. Foremost among these are those most hopeless of beings who are handicapped by having some measure which they consider it absolutely necessary for the sake of their own future to "get through." One of these men will have a bill, for instance, appropriating a sum of money from the State Treasury to clear out a river, dam the outlet of a lake, or drain a marsh; it may be, although not usually so, proper enough in itself, but it is drawn up primarily in the interest of a certain set of his constitutents who have given him clearly to understand that his continuance in their good graces depends upon his success in passing the bill. He feels that he must get it through at all hazards; the bad men find this out, and tell him he must count on their opposition unless he consents also to help their measures; he resists at first, but sooner or later yields; and from that moment his fate is sealed,— so far as his ability to do any work of general good is concerned.

A still larger number of men are good enough in themselves, but are " owned " by third parties. Usually the latter are politicians who have absolute control of the district machine, or who are, at least, of very great importance in the political affairs of their district. A curious fact is that they are not invariably, though usually, of the same party as the member; for in some places, especially in the lower portions of the great cities, politics become purely a business, and in the squabbles for offices of emolument it becomes important for a local leader to have supporters among all the factions. When one of these supporters is sent to a legislative body, he is allowed to act with the rest of his party on what his chief regards as the unimportant questions of party or public interest, but he has to come in to heel at once when any matter arises touching the said chief's power, pocket, or influence.

Other members will be controlled by some wealthy private citizen who is not in politics, but who has business interests likely to be affected by legislation, and who is therefore, willing to subscribe heavily to the campaign expenses of an individual or of an association so as to insure the presence in Albany of some one who will give him information and assistance.

On one occasion there came before a committee of which I happened to be a member, a perfectly proper bill in the interest of a certain corporation; the majority of the committee, six in number, were thoroughly bad men, who opposed the measure with the hope of being paid to cease their opposition. When I consented to take charge of the bill, I had stipulated that not a penny should be paid to insure its passage. It, therefore, became necessary to see what pressure could be brought to bear on the recalcitrant members; and, accordingly, we had to find out who were the authors and sponsors of their political being. Three proved to be under the control of local statesmen of the same party as themselves, and of equally bad moral character; one was ruled by a politician of unsavory reputation from a different city; the fifth, a Democrat, was owned by a Republican Federal official; and the sixth by the president of a horse-car company. A couple of letters from these two magnates forced the last members mentioned to change front on the bill with suprising alacrity.

There are two classes of cases in which corrupt members get money. One is when a wealthy corporation buys through some measure which will be of great benefit to itself, although, perhaps, an injury to the public at large; the other is when a member introduces a bill hostile to some moneyed interest, with the expectation of being paid to let the matter drop. The latter, technically called a "strike," is much the most common; for, in spite of the outcry against them in legislative matters, corporations are more often sinned against than sinning. It is difficult, for reasons already given, in either case to convict the offending member, though we have very good laws against bribery. The reform has got to come from the people at large. It will be hard to make any very great improvement in the character of the legislators until respectable people become more fully awake to their duties, and until the newspapers become more truthful and less reckless in their statements.

It is not a pleasant task to have to draw one side of legislative life in such dark colors; but as the side exists,

and as the dark lines never can be rubbed out until we
have manfully acknowledged that they are there and
need rubbing out, it seems the falsest of false delicacy to
refrain from dwelling upon them. But it would be most
unjust to accept this partial truth as being the whole
truth. We blame the Legislature for many evils, the
ultimate cause for whose existence is to be found in our
own shortcomings.

THE OTHER SIDE OF THE PICTURE.

THERE is a much brighter side to the picture, and this
is the larger side, too. It would be impossible to get
together a body of more earnest, upright, and disinterested men than the band of legislators, largely young
men, who during the past three years have averted so
much evil and accomplished so much good at Albany.
They were able, at least partially, to put into actual
practice the theories that had long been taught by the
intellectual leaders of the country. And the life of a
legislator who is earnest in his efforts to faithfully perform his duty as a public servant, is harassing and labo-
rious to the last degree. He is kept at work from eight
to fourteen hours a day; he is obliged to incur the bit-
terest hostility of a body of men as powerful as they are
uuscrupulous, who are always on the watch to find out,
or to make out, anything in his private or his public life
which can be used against him; and he has on his side
either a but partially roused public opinion, or else a
public opinion roused, it is true, but only blindly conscious of the evil from which it suffers, and alike ignorant
and unwilling to avail itself of the proper remedy.

This body of legislators, who, at any rate, worked honestly for what they thought right, were, as a whole, quite unselfish, and were not treated particularly well by their people. Most of them soon got to realize the fact that if they wished to enjoy their brief space of political life (and most though not all of them did enjoy it), they would have to make it a rule never to consider, in deciding how to vote upon any question, how their vote would affect their own political prospects. No man can do good service in the Legislature as long as he is worrying over the effect of his actions upon his own future. After having learned this, most of them got on very happily indeed. As a rule, and where no matter of principle is involved, a member is bound to represent the views of those who have elected him ; but there are times when the voice of the people is anything but the voice of God, and then a conscientious man is equally bound to disregard it.

In the long run, and on the average, the public will usually do justice to its representatives ; but it is a very rough, uneven, and long-delayed justice. That is, judging from what I have myself seen of the way in which members were treated by their constituents, I should say that the chances of an honest man being retained in public life were about ten per cent. better than if he were dishonest, other things being equal. This is not a showing very creditable to us as a people ; and the explanation is to be found in the shortcomings peculiar to the different classes of our honest and respectable voters,— shortcomings which may be briefly outlined.

SHORTCOMINGS OF THE PEOPLE WHO SHOULD
TAKE PART IN POLITICAL WORK.

THE people of means in all great cities have in times past shamefully neglected their political duties, and have been contemptuously disregarded by the professional politicians in consequence. A number of them will get together in a large hall, will vociferously demand "reform," as if it were some concrete substance which could be handed out to them in slices, and will then disband with a feeling of the most serene self-satisfaction, and the belief that they have done their entire duty as citizens and members of the community. It is an actual fact that four out of five of our wealthy and educated men, of those who occupy what is called good social position, are really ignorant of the nature of a caucus or a primary meeting, and never attend either; and this is specially true of the young men. Now, under our form of government, no man can accomplish anything by himself; he must work in combination with others; and the men of whom we are speaking will never carry their proper weight in the political affairs of the country until they have formed themselves into some organization, or else, which would be better, have joined some of the organizations already existing. But there seems often to be a certain lack of virility, an unmanly absence of the robuster virtues, in our educated men, which makes them shrink from the struggle and the inevitable contact with rude and unprincipled politicians (who often must be very roughly handled before they can be forced to behave), which must needs accompany all participation in

American political life. Another reason why this class
is not of more consequence in politics, is that it is often
really out of sympathy—or, at least, its more conspicuous
members are—with the feelings and interests of the great
mass of the American people ; for it is a sad and discred-
itable fact that it is in this class that what has been
recently most aptly termed the " colonial" spirit still
survives. There sometimes crops out among our educated men in politics the same curious feeling of dependence upon foreign opinion that makes our young men
of fashion drive clumsy vehicles of English model, rather
than the better-built and lighter American ones ; and
that causes a certain section of our minor novelists to
write the most emasculated nonsense that ever flowed
from American pens. Until this survival of the spirit of
colonial dependence is dead, those in whom it exists will
serve chiefly as laughing-stocks to the shrewd, humorous,
and prejudiced people who form nine-tenths of our body-
politic, and whose chief characteristics are their intensely
American habits of thought, and their surly intolerance
of anything like subservience to outside and foreign
influences.

From different causes, the laboring classes, thoroughly
honest of heart, often fail to appreciate honesty in their
representatives. They are frequently not well informed
in regard to the character of the latter, and they are apt
to be led aside by the loud professions of the so-called
labor reformers, who are always promising to procure by
legislation the advantages which can only come to working men, or to any other men, by their individual
or united energy, intelligence, and forethought. Very

much has been accomplished by legislation for laboring men, by procuring mechanics' lien laws, factory laws, etc.; and hence it often comes that they think legislation can accomplish all things for them, and it is only natural, for instance, that a certain proportion of their number should adhere to the demagogue who votes for a law to double the rate of wages, rather than to the honest man who opposes it. When people are struggling for the necessaries of existence, and vaguely feel, whether rightly or wrongly, that they are also struggling against an unjustly ordered system of life, it is hard to convince them of the truth that an ounce of performance on their own part is worth a ton of legislative promises to change in some mysterious manner that life-system.

In the country districts justice to a member is somewhat more apt to be done. When, as is so often the case, it is not done, the cause is usually to be sought for in the numerous petty jealousies and local rivalries which are certain to exist in any small community whose interests are narrow and most of whose members are acquainted with each other; and besides this, our country vote is essentially a Bourbon or Tory vote, being very slow to receive new ideas, very tenacious of old ones, and hence inclined to look with suspicion upon any one who tries to shape his course according to some standard differing from that which is already in existence.

The actual work of procuring the passage of a bill through the Legislature is in itself far from slight. The hostility of the actively bad has to be discounted in advance, and the indifference of the passive majority, who are neither very good nor very bad, has to be overcome. This can usually be accomplished only by stirring up their constituencies; and so, besides the constant watchfulness over the course of the measure through both houses and the continual debating and parliamentary fencing which is necessary, it is also indispensable to get the people of districts not directly affected by the bill alive to its importance, so as to induce their representatives to vote for it. Thus, when the bill to establish a State park at Niagara was on its passage, it was found that the great majority of the country members were opposed to it, fearing that it might conceal some land-jobbing scheme, and also fearing that their constituents, whose vice is not extravagance, would not countenance so great an expenditure of public money. It was of no use arguing with the members, and instead the country newspapers were flooded with letters, pamphlets were circulated, visits and personal appeals were made, until a sufficient number of these members changed front to enable us to get the lacking votes.

LIFE IN THE LEGISLATURE.

As already said, some of us who usually acted together took a great deal of genuine enjoyment out of our experience at Albany. We liked the excitement and perpetual conflict, the necessity for putting forth all our powers to reach our ends, and the feeling that we were really being of some use in the world; and if we were often both saddened and angered by the vicious-ness and ignorance of some of our colleagues, yet, in return, the latter many times furnished us unwittingly a

good deal of amusement by their preposterous actions
and speeches. Some of these are really too good to be
lost, and are accordingly given below. The names and
circumstances, of course, have been so changed as to prevent the possibility of the real heroes of them being recognized. It must be understood that they stand for the
exceptional and not the ordinary workings of the average
legislative intellect. I have heard much more sound
sense than foolishness talked in Albany, but to record
the former would only bore the reader. And we must
bear in mind that while the ignorance of some of our
representatives warrants our saying that they should not
be in the Legislature, it does not at all warrant our condemning the system of government which permits them
to be sent there. There is no system so good that it has
not some disadvantages. The only way to teach Paddy
how to govern himself, and the only way to teach Sambo
how to save himself from oppression, is to give each the
full rights possessed by other American citizens ; and it
is not to be wondered at if they at first show themselves
unskilful in the exercise of these rights. It has been
my experience moreover in the Legislature that when
Paddy does turn out really well, there are very few
native Americans indeed who do better. There were no
better legislators in Albany than the two young Irishmen
who successively represented one of the districts of
Kings County; and when I had to name a committee
which was to do the most difficult, dangerous, and important work that came before the Legislature at all during my presence in it, I chose three of my four colleagues from among those of my fellow legislators who

were Irish either by birth or descent. The best friend I have ever had or hope to have in politics, and the most disinterested, is an Irishman, and is also as genuine and good an American citizen as is to be found within the United States.

A good many of the Yankees in the house would blunder time and again ; but their blunders were generally merely stupid and not at all amusing, while, on the contrary, the errors of those who were of Milesian extraction always possessed a most refreshing originality.

INCIDENTS OF LEGISLATIVE EXPERIENCE.

IN 1882 the Democrats in the house had a clear majority, but were for a long time unable to effect an organization, owing to a faction-fight in their own ranks between the Tammany and anti-Tammany members, each side claiming the lion's share of the spoils. After a good deal of bickering, the anti-Tammany men drew up a paper containing a series of propositions, and submitted it to their opponents, with the prefatory remark, in writing, that it was an *ultimatum*. The Tammany members were at once summoned to an indignation meeting, their feelings closely resembling those of the famous fish-wife whom O'Connell called a parallelopipedon. None of them had any very accurate idea as to what the word *ultimatum* meant; but that it was intensely offensive, not to say abusive, in its nature, they did not question for a moment. It was felt that some equivalent and equally strong term by which to call Tammany's proposed counter address must be found immediately; but, as the Latin vocabulary of the members was limited, it was some time before a suitable term was forthcoming. Finally, by a happy inspiration, some gentlemen of classical education remembered the phrase *"ipse dixit"*; it was at once felt to be the very phrase required by the peculiar exigencies of the case, and next day the reply appeared, setting forth with self-satisfied gravity that, in response to the County Democracy's *"ultimatum,"* Tammany herewith produced her *"ipse dixit."* Some of us endeavored to persuade the County Democratic leaders to issue a counter-blast, which could be styled either a *sine qua non* or a *tempus fugit*, according to the taste of the authors; but our efforts were not successful, and the *ipse dixit* remained unanswered.

Nor is it only Latin terms that sometimes puzzle our city politicians. A very able and worthy citizen, Mr. D., had on one occasion, before a legislative committee, advocated the restriction of the powers of the Board of Aldermen, instancing a number of occasions when they had been guilty of gross misconduct, and stating that in several other instances their conduct had been "identical" with that of which he had already given examples. Shortly afterwards the mayor nominated him for some office, but the aldermen refused to confirm him, one of them giving as his reason that Mr. D. had used "abusive and indecorous language" about the Board. On being cross-examined as to what he referred to, he stated that he had heard "with his own ears" Mr. D. call the alderman "identical"; and to the further remark that "identical" could scarcely be called either abusive or indecorous, he responded triumphantly that the aldermen were the best judges of matters affecting their own dignity.   Mr. D.'s nomination remained unconfirmed.

Shortly afterwards the aldermen fell foul of one of their own number, who, in commenting on some action of the Board, remarked that it was robbing Peter to pay Paul.   Down came the gavel of the acting president, while he informed the startled speaker that he would not tolerate blasphemous language from any one.   " But it was not blasphemous," returned the offender.   " Well, if it wasn't, it was vulgar, and that's worse," responded the president, with dignity ; and the admiring Board sustained him with practical unanimity in his position of censor-extraordinary over aldermanic morals.

Public servants of higher grade than aldermen sometimes give adjectives a wider meaning than would be found in the dictionary.   In many parts of the United States, owing to a curious series of historical associations (which, by the way, would be interesting to trace out), anything foreign and un-English is called " Dutch," and it was in this sense that a West Virginian member of a recent Congress used the term when, in speaking in favor of a tariff on works of art, he told of the reluctance with which he saw the productions of native artists exposed to competition " with Dutch daubs from Italy "; a sentence pleasing alike from its alliteration and from its bold disregard of geographic trivialities.

Often an orator of this sort will have his attention attracted by some high-sounding word, which he has not before seen, and which he treasures up to use in his next rhetorical flight, without regard to the exact meaning.

3

There was a laboring man's advocate in the last Legislature, one of whose efforts attracted a good deal of attention from his magnificent heedlessness of technical accuracy in the use of similes. He was speaking against the convict contract-labor system, and wound up an already sufficiently remarkable oration with the still more startling ending that the system "was a vital cobra which was swamping the lives of the laboring men." Now, he had evidently carefully put together the sentence beforehand, and the process of mental synthesis by which he built it up must have been curious. "Vital" was, of course, used merely as an adjective of intensity; he was a little uncertain in his ideas as to what a "cobra" was, but took it for granted that it was some terrible manifestation of nature, possibly hostile to man, like a volcano, or a cyclone, or Niagara, for instance; then "swamping" was chosen as describing an operation very likely to be performed by Niagara, or a cyclone, or a cobra; and, behold, the sentence was complete.

Sometimes a common phrase will be given a new meaning. Thus, the mass of legislation is strictly local in its character. Over a thousand bills come up for consideration in the course of a session, but a very few of which affect the interests of the State at large. The latter and the more important private bills are, or ought to be, carefully studied by each member; but it is a physical impossibility for any one man to examine the countless local bills of small importance. For these we have to trust to the member for the district affected, and when one comes up the response to any inquiry about it is usually, "Oh, it's a local bill, affecting so-and-so's district ; he is responsible for it." By degrees, some of the members get to use "local" in the sense of unimportant, and a few of the assemblymen of doubtful honesty gradually come to regard it as meaning a bill of no pecuniary interest to themselves. There was a smug little rascal in one of the last Legislatures, who might have come out of one of Lever's novels. He was undoubtedly a bad case, but had a genuine sense of humor, and his "bulls" made him the delight of the house. One day I came in late, just as a bill was being voted on, and meeting my friend, hailed him, " Hello, Pat, what's up? what's this they're voting on?" to which Pat replied, with contemptuous indifference to the subject, but with a sly twinkle in his eye, "Oh, some unimportant measure, sorr ; some local bill or other—*a constitutional amendment !* "

The old Dublin Parliament never listened to a better specimen of a bull than was contained in the speech of a very genial and pleasant friend of mine, a really finished orator, who, in the excitement attendant upon receiving the governor's message vetoing the famous five-cent fare bill, uttered the following sentence : " Mr. Speaker, I recognize the hand that crops out in that veto ; *I have heard it before !* "

One member rather astonished us one day by his use of "shibboleth." He had evidently concluded that this was merely a more elegant synonym of the good old word shillalah, and in reproving a colleague for opposing a bill to increase the salaries of public laborers, he said, very impressively, " The trouble wid the young man is, that he uses the wurrd economy as a shibboleth, wherewith to strike the working man." Afterwards he changed the metaphor, and spoke of a number of us as using the word "reform" as a shibboleth, behind which to cloak our evil intentions.

A mixture of classical and constitutional misinformation was displayed a few sessions past in the State Senate, before I was myself a member of the Legislature. It was on the occasion of that annual nuisance, the debate upon the Catholic Protectory item of the Supply Bill. Every year some one who is desirous of bidding for the Catholic vote introduces this bill, which appropriates a sum of varying dimensions for the support of the Catholic Protectory, an excellent institution, but one which has no right whatever to come to the State for support; each year the insertion of the item is opposed by a small number of men, including the more liberal Catholics themselves, on proper grounds, and by a larger number from simple bigotry—a fact which was shown two years ago, when many of the most bitter opponents of this measure cheerfully supported a similar and equally objectionable one in aid of a Protestant institution. On the occasion referred to there were two senators, both Celtic gentlemen, who were rivals for the leadership of the minority; one of them a stout, red-faced little man, who went by the name of "Commodore," owing to his having seen service in the navy; while the other was a dapper, voluble fellow, who had at one time been on a civic commission and was always called the "Counselor." A mild-mannered countryman was opposing the insertion of the item on the ground (perfectly just, by the way) that it was unconstitutional, and he dwelt upon this objection at some length. The Counselor, who knew nothing of the constitution, except that it was continually being quoted against all of his favorite projects, fidgeted about for some time, and at last jumped up to know if he might ask the gentleman a question. The latter said, "Yes," and the Counselor went on, "I'd like to know if the gintleman has ever personally seen the Catholic Protectorce?" "No, I haven't," said the astonished countryman. "Then, phwat do you mane by talking about its being unconstitootional, I'd like to know? It's no more unconstitootional than you are! Not one bit! I know it, for I've been and seen it, and that's more than you've done." Then, turning to the house, with slow and withering sarcasm, he added, "The throuble wid the gintleman is that he okkipies what lawyers would call a kind of a quasi-position upon this bill," and sat down amid the applause of his followers.

His rival, the Commodore, felt he had gained altogether too much glory from the encounter, and after the nonplussed countryman had taken his seat, he stalked solemnly over to the desk of the elated Counselor, looked at him majestically for a moment, and said, "You'll excuse my mentioning, sorr, that the gintleman who has just sat down knows more law in a wake than you do in a month; and more than that, Counselor Shaunnessy, phwat do you mane by quotin' Latin on the flure of this house, *when you don't know the alpha and omayga of the language!*" and back he walked, leaving the Counselor in humiliated submission behind him.

The counselor was always falling foul of the Constitu-

•
tion. Once, when defending one of his bills which made
a small but wholly indefinable appropriation of state
money for a private purpose, he asserted "that the Constitution didn't touch little things like that;" and on
another occasion he remarked in my presence that he
"never allowed the Constitution to come between
friends."

The Commodore was at that time chairman of a Senate committee, before which there sometimes came questions affecting the interests or supposed interests of
labor. The committee was hopelessly bad in its composition, the members being either very corrupt or exceedingly inefficient. The Commodore generally kept order
with a good deal of dignity ; indeed, when, as not infre-
quently happened, he had looked upon the rye that was
flavored with lemon-peel, his sense of personal dignity
grew till it became fairly majestic, and he ruled the committee with a rod of iron. At one time a bill had been
introduced (one of the several score of preposterous
measures that annually make their appearance purely for
purposes of buncombe), by whose terms all laborers in
the public works of great cities were to receive three
dollars a day—double the market price of labor. To
this bill, by the way, an amendment was afterwards
offered in the house by some gentleman with a sense of
humor, which was to make it read that all the inhabi-
tants of great cities were to receive three dollars a day,
and the privilege of laboring on the public works if they
chose ; the original author of the bill questioning doubt-
fully if the amendment "didn't make the measure a
trifle too sweeping." The measure was, of course, of no

consequence whatever to the genuine laboring men, but
was of interest to the professional labor agitators; and a
body of the latter requested leave to appear before the
committee. This was granted, but on the appointed day
the chairman turned up in a condition of such portentous
dignity as to make it evident that he had been on a
spree of protracted duration. Down he sat at the head
of the table, and glared at the committeemen, while the
latter, whose faces would not have looked amiss in a
rogues' gallery, cowered before him. The first speaker
was a typical professional laboring man; a sleek, oily
little fellow, with a black mustache, who had never done
a stroke of work in his life. He felt confident that the
Commodore would favor him,—a confidence soon to be
rudely shaken,—and began with a deprecatory smile :

"Humble though I am——"

Rap, rap, went the chairman's gavel, and the following
dialogue occurred :

Chairman (with dignity). "What's that you said you
were, sir ?"

Professional Workingman (decidedly taken aback).
"I—I said I was humble, sir ?"

Chairman (reproachfully). "Are you an American
citizen, sir ?"

P. W. "Yes, sir."

Chairman (with emphasis). "Then you're the equal
of any man in this State! Then you're the equal of any
man on this committee! *Don't let me hear you call your-
self humble again! Go on, sir !*"

After this warning the advocate managed to keep
clear of the rocks until, having worked himself up to

quite a pitch of excitement, he incautiously exclaimed,
" But the poor man has no friends! " which brought the
Commodore down on him at once. Rap, rap, went his
gavel, and he scowled grimly at the offender while he
asked with deadly deliberation :

" What did you say that time, sir? "

P. W. (hopelessly). " I said the poor man had no
friends, sir."

Chairman (with sudden fire). "Then you lied, sir! I
am the poor man's friend! so are my colleagues, sir! "
(Here the rogues' gallery tried to look benevolent.)
" Speak the truth, sir! " (with sudden change from the
manner admonitory to the manner mandatory). " Now,
you, sit down quick, or get out of this somehow! "

This put an end to the sleek gentleman, and his place
was taken by a fellow-professional of another type—a
great, burly man, who would talk to you on private
matters in a perfectly natural tone of voice, but who, the
minute he began to speak of the Wrongs (with a capital
W) of Labor (with a capital L), bellowed as if he had
been a bull of Bashan. The Commodore, by this time
pretty far gone, eyed him malevolently, swaying to and
fro in his chair. However, the first effect of the fellow's
oratory was soothing rather than otherwise, and produced the unexpected result of sending the chairman
fast asleep sitting bolt upright. But in a minute or two,
as the man warmed up to his work, he gave a peculiarly
resonant howl which waked the Commodore up. The
latter came to himself with a jerk, looked fixedly at the
audience, caught sight of the speaker, remembered hav-

ing seen him before, forgot that he had been asleep, and concluded that it must have been on some previous day. Hammer, hammer, went the gavel, and—

"I've seen you before, sir!"

"You have not," said the man.

"Don't tell me I lie, sir!" responded the Commodore, with sudden ferocity. "You've addressed this committee on a previous day!"

"I've never—" began the man; but the Commodore broke in again:

"Sit down, sir! The dignity of the chair must be preserved! No man shall speak to this committee twice. The committee stands adjourned." And with that he stalked majestically out of the room, leaving the committee and the delegation to gaze sheepishly into each other's faces.

OUTSIDERS.

AFTER all, outsiders furnish quite as much fun as the legislators themselves. The number of men who persist in writing one letters of praise, abuse, and advice on every conceivable subject is appalling; and the writers are of every grade, from the lunatic and the criminal up. The most difficult to deal with are the men with hobbies. There is the Protestant fool, who thinks that our liberties are menaced by the machinations of the Church of Rome; and his companion idiot, who wants legislation against all secret societies, especially the Masons. Then there are the believers in "isms," of whom the women-suffragists stand in the first rank. Now, to the horror of my relatives, I have always been a believer in woman's rights, but I must confess I have never seen such a hopelessly impracticable set of persons as the woman-suffragists who came up to Albany to get legislation. They simply would not draw up their measures in proper form ; when I pointed out to one of them that their proposed bill was drawn up in direct defiance of certain of the sections of the Constitution of the State he blandly replied that he did not care at all for that, because the measure had been drawn up so as to be in accord with the Constitution of Heaven. There was no answer to this beyond the very obvious one that Albany was in no way akin to Heaven. The ultra-temperance people—not the moderate and sensible ones—are quite as impervious to common sense.

A member's correspondence is sometimes amusing. A member receives shoals of letters of advice, congratulation, entreaty, and abuse, half of them anonymous. Most of these are stupid, but one received by a friend broke the monotony by the charming frankness with which it began, " Mr. So-and-so—Sir : Oh, you goggle-eyed liar ! "—a sentence which thus combined a graphic estimate of my friend's moral worth together with a delicate allusion to the fact that he wore eye-glasses.

I had some constant correspondents. One lady in the western part of the State wrote me a weekly disquisition on woman's rights. A Buffalo clergyman spent two years on a one-sided correspondence about prohibition. A gentleman of ——— wrote me such a stream of essays and requests about the charter of that city that I feared he would drive me into a lunatic asylum ; but he anticipated matters by going into one himself. A New York at regular intervals sent up a request that I would "reintroduce" the Dongan charter, which had lapsed about the year 1720. A gentleman interested in a proposed law to protect primaries took to telegraphing daily questions as to its progress—a habit of which I broke him by sending in response telegrams of several hundred words each, which I was careful not to prepay.

There are certain legislative actions which must be taken in a purely Pickwickian sense. Notable among these are the resolutions of sympathy for the alleged oppressed patriots and peoples of Europe. These are generally directed against England, as there exists in the lower strata of political life an Anglophobia quite as objectionable, though not as contemptible, as the Anglomania at present prevailing in the higher social circles.

As a rule, these resolutions are to be classed as simply *bouffe* affairs; they are commonly introduced by some ambitious legislator—often I regret to say, a native American—who has a large foreign vote in his district (the famous O'Donnell resolution in Congress is a particularly unfortunate recent instance). During my term of service in the Legislature, resolutions were introduced demanding the recall of Minister Lowell, assailing the Czar for his conduct towards the Russian Jews, sympathizing with the Land League and the Dutch Boers, etc., etc.; the passage of each of which we strenuously and usually successfully opposed, on the ground that while we would warmly welcome any foreigner who came here, and in good faith assumed the duties of American citizenship, we had a right to demand in return that he should not bring any of his race or national antipathies into American political life. Resolutions of this character are sometimes undoubtedly proper, but are in nine cases out of ten wholly unjustifiable. An instance of this sort of thing which took place not at Albany may be cited. Recently the Board of Aldermen of one of our great cities received a stinging rebuke, which it is to be feared the aldermanic intellect was too dense to fully appreciate. The aldermen passed a resolution "condemning" the Czar of Russia for his conduct towards his fellow-citizens of Hebrew faith, and "demanding" that he should forthwith treat them better; this was forwarded to the Russian Minister with a request that it be sent to the Czar. It came back forty-eight hours afterwards, with a note on the back by one of the under-secretaries of the legation, to the effect that as he was not aware that Russia had any diplomatic relations with this particular Board of Aldermen, and as, indeed, Russia was not officially cognizant of their existence, and, moreover, was wholly indifferent to their opinions on any conceivable subject, he herewith returned them their kind communication.

In concluding, I would say that while there is so much evil at Albany, and so much reason for our exerting ourselves to bring about a better state of things, yet there is no cause for being disheartened or for thinking that it is hopeless to expect improvement. On the contrary, the standard of legislative morals is certainly higher than it was fifteen years ago or twenty-five years ago, and, judging by appearances, it seems likely that it will continue slowly and by fits and starts to improve in the future; keeping pace exactly with the gradual awakening of the popular mind to the necessity of having honest and intelligent representatives in the State Legislature.

I have had opportunity of knowing something about the workings of but a few of our other State Legislatures; from what I have seen and heard, I should say that we stand about on a par with those of Pennsylvania, Maryland, and Illinois, above that of Louisiana, and below those of Vermont, Massachusetts, Rhode Island, and Wyoming, as well as below the National Legislature at Washington. But the moral status of a legislative body, especially in the West, often varies widely from year to year.

MACHINE POLITICS IN NEW YORK CITY.

IN New York city, as in most of our other great municipalities, the direction of political affairs has been for many years mainly in the hands of a class of men who make politics their regular business and means of livelihood. These men are able to keep their grip only by means of the singularly perfect way in which they have succeeded in organizing their respective parties and factions; and it is in consequence of the clock-work regularity and efficiency with which these several organizations play their parts, alike for good and for evil, that they have been nicknamed by outsiders "machines," while the men who take part in and control, or, as they would themselves say, "run" them, form now a well-recognized and fairly well-defined class in the community, and are familiarly known as machine politicians. It may be of interest to sketch in outline some of the characteristics of these men and of their machines, the methods by which and the objects for which they work, and the reasons for their success in the political field.

The terms machine and machine politician are now undoubtedly used ordinarily in a reproachful sense; but it does not at all follow that this sense is always the right one. On the contrary, the machine is often a very powerful instrument for good; and a machine politician really desirous of doing honest work on behalf of the

46

community is fifty times as useful an ally as is the average philanthropic outsider. Indeed, it is of course true
that any political organization (and absolutely no good
work can be done in politics without an organization) is
a machine; and any man who perfects and uses this
organization is himself, to a certain extent, a machine
politician. In the rough, however, the feeling against
machine politics and politicians is tolerably well justified
by the facts, although this statement really reflects most
severely upon the educated and honest people who
largely hold themselves aloof from public life, and show
a curious incapacity for fulfilling their public duties.

The organizations that are commonly and distinctively
known as machines are those belonging to the two great
recognized parties, or to their factional subdivisions; and
the reason why the word machine has come to be used,
to a certain extent, as a term of opprobrium is to be
found in the fact that these organizations are now run by
the leaders very largely as business concerns to benefit
themselves and their followers, with little regard to the
community at large. This is natural enough. The men
having control and doing all the work have gradually
come to have the same feeling about politics that other
men have about the business of a merchant or manufacturer; it was too much to expect that if left entirely to
themselves they would continue disinterestedly to work
for the benefit of others. Many a machine politician
who is to-day a most unwholesome influence in our politics is in private life quite as respectable as any one else;
only he has forgotten that his business affects the state
at large, and, regarding it as merely his own private con-

cern, he has carried into it the same selfish spirit that actuates the majority of the mercantile community. A merchant or manufacturer works his business, as a rule, purely for his own benefit, without any regard whatever for the community at large; the merchant uses all his influence for a low tariff, and the manufacturer is even more strenuously in favor of protection, not at all from any theory of abstract right, but because of self-interest. Each views such a political question as the tariff, not from the standpoint of how it will affect the nation as a whole, but merely from that of how it will affect him personally; and private business is managed still less with a view to the well-being of the people at large. If a community were in favor of protection, but nevertheless permitted all the governmental machinery to fall into the hands of importing merchants, it would be small cause for wonder if the latter shaped the laws to suit themselves, and the chief blame, after all, would rest with the supine and lethargic majority which failed to have enough energy to take charge of their own affairs. Our machine politicians, in actual life, act in just this same way; their actions are almost always dictated by selfish motives, with but little regard for the people at large; they therefore need continually to be watched and opposed by those who wish to see good government. But, after all, it is hardly to be wondered at that they abuse power which is allowed to fall into their hands owing to the ignorance or timid indifference of those who by rights should themselves keep it.

In a society properly constituted for true democratic government—in a society such as that seen in many of our country towns, for example—machine rule is impossible. But in New York, as well as in most of our other great cities, the conditions favor the growth of ring or boss rule. The chief causes thus operating against good government are the moral and mental attitudes towards politics assumed by different sections of the voters. A large number of these are simply densely ignorant, and, of course, such are apt to fall under the influence of cunning leaders, and even if they do right, it is by hazard merely. The criminal class in a great city is always of some size, while what may be called the potentially-criminal class is still larger. Then there is a great class of laboring men, mostly of foreign birth or parentage, who at present both expect too much from legislation and yet at the same time realize too little how powerfully though indirectly they are affected by a bad or corrupt government. In many wards the overwhelming majority of the voters do not realize that heavy taxes fall ultimately upon them, and actually view with perfect complacency burdens laid by their representatives upon the tax-payers, and, if anything, approve of a hostile attitude towards the latter—having a vague feeling of hostility towards them as possessing more than their proper proportion of the world's good things, and sharing with most other human beings the capacity to bear with philosophic equanimity ills merely affecting one's neighbors. When powerfully roused on some financial, but still more on some sentimental question, this same laboring class will throw its enormous and usually decisive weight into the scale which it believes inclines to the right; but its members are often curiously and cyni-

4

cally indifferent to charges of corruption against favorite
heroes or demagogues, so long as these charges do not
imply betrayal of their own real or fancied interests.
Thus an alderman or assemblyman representing certain
wards may make as much money as he pleases out of
corporations without seriously jeopardizing his standing
with his constituents; but if he once, whether from
honest or dishonest motives, stands by a corporation
when the interests of the latter are supposed to conflict
with those of " the people," it is all up with him. These
voters are, moreover, very emotional; they value in a
public man what we are accustomed to consider virtues
only to be taken into account when estimating private
character. Thus, if a man is open-handed and warm-
hearted, they consider it as a fair offset to his being a
little bit shaky when it comes to applying the eighth
commandment to affairs of state. I have more than once
heard the statement, " He is very liberal to the poor,"
advanced as a perfectly satisfactory answer to the charge
that a certain public man was corrupt. Moreover, working men, whose lives are passed in one unceasing round
of narrow and monotonous toil, not unnaturally are
inclined to pay heed to the demagogues and professional
labor advocates who promise if elected to try to pass
laws to better their condition ; they are hardly prepared
to understand or approve the American doctrine of government, which is that the state has no business whatever to attempt to better the condition of a man or a set
of men, but has merely to see that no wrong is done him
or them by any one else, and that all alike are to have a
fair chance in the struggle for life—a struggle wherein, it

may as well at once be freely though sadly acknowledged, very many are bound to fail, no matter how
ideally perfect any given system of government may be.

Of course it must be remembered that all these general statements are subject to an immense number of
individual exceptions; there are tens of thousands of
men who work with their hands for their daily bread and
yet put into actual practice that sublime virtue of disinterested adherence to the right, even when it seems
likely merely to benefit others, and those others better
off than they themselves are; for they vote for honesty
and cleanliness, in spite of great temptation to do the
opposite, and in spite of their not seeing how any immediate benefit will result to themselves.

REASONS FOR THE NEGLECT OF PUBLIC DUTIES BY RESPECTABLE MEN IN EASY CIRCUMSTANCES.

THIS class is composed of the great bulk of the men
who range from well-to-do up to very rich; and of these
the former generally and the latter almost universally
neglect their political duties, for the most part rather
pluming themselves upon their good conduct if they so
much as vote on election day. This largely comes from
the tremendous wear and tension of life in our great
cities. Moreover, the men of small means with us are
usually men of domestic habits; and this very devotion
to home, which is one of their chief virtues, leads them
to neglect their public duties. They work hard, as
clerks, mechanics, small tradesmen, etc., all day long,
and when they get home in the evening they dislike to
go out. If they do go to a ward meeting, they find

themselves isolated, and strangers both to the men whom they meet and to the matter on which they have to act ; for in the city a man is quite as sure to know next to nothing about his neighbors as in the country he is to be intimately acquainted with them. In the country the people of a neighborhood, when they assemble in one of their local conventions, are already mutually well acquainted, and therefore able to act together with effect ; whereas in the city, even if the ordinary citizens do come out, they are totally unacquainted with one another, and are as helplessly unable to oppose the disciplined ranks of the professional politicians as is the case with a mob of freshmen in one of our colleges when in danger of being hazed by the sophomores. Moreover, the pressure of competition in city life is so keen that men often have as much as they can do to attend to their own affairs, and really hardly have the leisure to look after those of the public. Indeed, the general tendency everywhere is toward the specialization of functions, and this holds good as well in politics as elsewhere.

The reputable private citizens of small means thus often neglect to attend to their public duties because to do so would perhaps interfere with their private business. This is bad enough, but the case is worse with the really wealthy, who still more generally neglect these same duties, partly because not to do so would interfere with their pleasure, and partly from a combination of other motives, all of them natural but none of them creditable. A successful merchant, well dressed, pompous, self-important, unused to any life outside of the counting-room, and accustomed because of his very success to be treated

with deferential regard, as one who stands above the
common run of humanity, naturally finds it very unpleasant to go to a caucus or primary where he has to stand
on an equal footing with his groom and day-laborers, and
indeed may discover that the latter, thanks to their fac-
ulty for combination, are rated higher in the scale of
political importance than he is himself. In all the large
cities of the North the wealthier, or, as they would prefer
to style themselves, the " upper " classes, tend distinctly
towards the bourgeois type ; and an individual in the
bourgeois stage of development, while honest, industri-
ous, and virtuous, is also not unapt to be a miracle of
timid and short-sighted selfishness. The commercial
classes are only too likely to regard everything merely
from the stand-point of " Does it pay? " and many a
merchant does not take any part in politics because he is
short-sighted enough to think that it will pay him better
to attend purely to making money, and too selfish to be
willing to undergo any trouble for the sake of abstract
duty ; while the younger men of this type are too much
engrossed in their various social pleasures to be willing
to give their time to anything else. It is also unfortunately true, especially throughout New England and the
Middle States, that the general tendency among people
of culture and high education has been to neglect and
even to look down upon the rougher and manlier virtues,
so that an advanced state of intellectual development is
too often associated with a certain effeminacy of character. Our more intellectual men often shrink from the
raw coarseness and the eager struggle of political life as
if they were women. Now, however refined and virtuous

a man may be, he is yet entirely out of place in the American body-politic unless he is himself of sufficiently coarse fiber and virile character to be more angered than hurt by an insult or injury ; the timid good form a most useless as well as a most despicable portion of the community. Again, when a man is heard objecting to taking part in politics because it is "low," he may be set down as either a fool or a coward ; it would be quite as sensible for a militiaman to advance the same statement as an excuse for refusing to assist in quelling a riot. Many cultured men neglect their political duties simply because they are too delicate to have the element of "strike back" in their natures, and because they have an unmanly fear of being forced to stand up for their own rights when threatened with abuse or insult. Such are the conditions which give the machine men their chance ; and they have been able to make the most possible out of this chance,—first, because of the perfection to which they have brought their machinery, and, second, because of the social character of their political organizations.

ORGANIZATION AND WORK OF THE MACHINES.

THE machinery of any one of our political bodies is always rather complicated ; and its politicians invariably endeavor to keep it so, because, their time being wholly given to it, they are able to become perfectly familiar with all its workings, while the average outsider becomes more and more helpless in proportion as the organization is less and less simple. Besides some others of minor importance, there are at present in New York three great political organizations, *viz.*, those of the regular Republicans, of the County Democracy, and of Tammany Hall, that of the last being perhaps the most perfect, viewed from a machine stand-point. Although with wide differences in detail, all these bodies are organized upon much the same general plan; and one description may be taken, in the rough, as applying to all. There is a large central committee, composed of numerous delegates from the different assembly districts, which decides upon the various questions affecting the party as a whole in the county and city; and then there are the various organizations in the assembly districts themselves, which are the real sources of strength, and with which alone it is necessary to deal. There are different rules for the admission to the various district primaries and caucuses of the voters belonging to the respective parties; but in almost every case the real work is done and the real power held by a small knot of men, who in turn pay a greater or less degree of fealty to a single boss.

The mere work to be done on election day and in preparing for it forms no slight task. There is an association in each assembly district, with its president, secretary, treasurer, executive committee, etc.; these call the primaries and caucuses, arrange the lists of the delegates to the various nominating conventions, raise funds for campaign purposes, and hold themselves in communication with their central party organizations. At the primaries in each assembly district a full set of delegates are chosen to nominate assemblymen and aldermen, while others are chosen to go to the State, county, and congressional conventions. Before election day many thousands of complete sets of the party ticket are printed, folded, and put together, or, as it is called, "bunched." A single bundle of these ballots is then sent to every voter in the district, while thousands are reserved for distribution at the polls. In every election precinct—there are probably twenty or thirty in each assembly district—a captain and from two to a dozen subordinates are appointed. These have charge of the actual giving out of the ballots at the polls. On election day they are at their places long before the hour set for voting; each party has a wooden booth, looking a good deal like a sentry-box, covered over with flaming posters containing the names of their nominees, and the "workers" cluster around these as centers. Every voter as he approaches is certain to be offered a set of tickets; usually these sets are "straight," that is, contain all the nominees of one party, but frequently crooked work will be done, and some one candidate will get his own ballots bunched with the rest of those of the opposite party. Each captain of a district is generally paid a certain sum of money, greater or less according to his ability as a politician or according to his power of serving the boss or machine. Nominally this money goes in paying the subordinates and in what are vaguely termed "campaign expenses," but as a matter of fact it is in many instances simply pocketed by the recipient; indeed, very little of the large sums of money annually spent by candidates to bribe voters actually reaches the voters supposed to be bribed. The money thus furnished is procured either by subscriptions from rich outsiders, or by assessments upon the candidates themselves; formerly much was also obtained from office-holders, but this is now prohibited by law. A great deal of money is also spent in advertising, placarding posters, paying for public meetings, and organizing and uniforming members to take part in some huge torchlight procession—this last particular form of idiocy being one peculiarly dear to the average American political mind. Candidates for very lucrative positions are often assessed really huge sums, in order to pay for the extravagant methods by which our canvasses are conducted. Before a legislative committee of which I was a member, the Register of New York county blandly testified under oath that he had forgotten whether his expenses during his canvass had been over or under fifty thousand dollars. It must be remembered that even now—and until recently the evil was very much greater—the rewards paid to certain public officials are out of all proportion to the services rendered; and in such cases the active managing politicians feel that they have a right to exact the heaviest possible toll from the candidate, to help pay the army of hungry heelers who do their bidding. Thus, before the same committee mentioned above, the County Clerk testified that his income was very nearly eighty thousand a year, but with refreshing frankness admitted that his own position was practically merely that of a figure-head, and that all the work was done by his deputy, on a small fixed salary. As the County Clerk's term is three years, he should nominally receive nearly a quarter of a million dollars; but as a matter of fact two-thirds of the money probably goes to the political organizations with which he is connected. The enormous emoluments of such officers are, of course, most effective in debauching politics. They bear no relation whatever to the trifling quantity of work done, and the chosen candidate readily recognizes what is the exact truth,—namely, that the benefit of his service is expected to enure to his party allies, and not to the citizens at large. Thus, one of the county officers who came before the above mentioned committee, testified with a naïve openness which was appalling, in answer to what was believed to be a purely formal question as to whether he performed his public duties faithfully, that he did so perform them whenever they did not conflict with his political duties! —meaning thereby, as he explained, attending to his local organizations, seeing politicians, fixing primaries, bailing out those of his friends (apparently by no means few in number) who got hauled up before a justice of the peace, etc., etc. This man's statements were valuable because, being a truthful person and of such dense ignorance that he was at first wholly unaware his testimony was in any way remarkable, he really tried to tell things as they were ; and it had evidently never occurred to him that he was not expected by every one to do just as he had been doing,—that is, to draw a large salary for himself, to turn over a still larger fund to his party allies, and conscientiously to endeavor, as far as he could, by the free use of his time and influence, to satisfy the innumerable demands made upon him by the various small-fry politicians.

"HEELERS."

THE "heelers," or "workers," who stand at the polls, and are paid in the way above described, form a large part of the rank and file composing each organization. There are, of course, scores of them in each assembly district association, and, together with the almost equally numerous class of federal, State, or local paid office-holders (except in so far as these last have been cut out by the operations of the civil-service reform laws), they form the bulk of the men by whom the machine is run, the bosses of great and small degree chiefly merely oversee the work and supervise the deeds of their henchmen. The organization of a party in our city is really much like that of an army. There is one great central boss, assisted by some trusted and able lieutenants; these communicate with the different district bosses, whom they alternately bully and assist. The district boss in turn has a number of half subordinates, half allies, under him; and these latter choose the captains of the election districts, etc., and come into contact with the common heelers. The more stupid and ignorant the common heelers are, and the more implicitly they obey orders, the greater becomes the effectiveness of the machine. An ideal machine has for its officers men of marked force, cunning and unscrupulous, and for its common soldiers men who may be either corrupt or moderately honest, but who must be of low intelligence. This is the reason why such a large proportion of the members of every political machine are recruited from the lower grades of the foreign population. These henchmen obey unhesitatingly the orders of their chiefs, both at the primary or caucus and on election day, receiving regular rewards for so doing, either in employment procured for them or else in money outright. Of course it is by no means true that these men are all actuated merely by mercenary motives. The great majority entertain also a real feeling of allegiance towards the party to which they belong, or towards the political chief whose fortunes they follow ; and many work entirely without pay and purely for what they believe to be right. Indeed, an experienced politician always greatly prefers to have under him men whose hearts are in their work and upon whose unbribed devotion and intelligence he can rely ; but unfortunately he finds in most cases that their exertions have to be seconded by others which are prompted by motives far more mixed.

All of these men, whether paid or not, make a business of political life and are thoroughly at home among the obscure intrigues that go to make up so much of it ; and consequently, they have quite as much the advantage when pitted against amateurs as regular soldiers have when matched against militiamen. But their numbers, though absolutely large, are, relatively to the entire community, so small that some other cause must be taken into consideration in order to account for the commanding position occupied by the machine and the machine politicians in public life. This other determining cause is to be found in the fact that all these machine associations have a social as well as a political

side, and that a large part of the political life of every
leader or boss is also identical with his social life.

THE SOCIAL SIDE OF MACHINE POLITICS.

THE political associations of the various districts are
not organized merely at the approach of election day ;
on the contrary, they exist throughout the year, and
for the greater part of the time are to a great extent
merely social clubs. To a large number of the men who
belong to them they are the chief social rallying-point.
These men congregate in the association building in the
evening to smoke, drink beer, and play cards, precisely
as the wealthier men gather in the clubs whose purpose
is avowedly social and not political—such as the Union,
University, and Knickerbocker. Politics thus becomes a
pleasure and relaxation as well as a serious pursuit.
The different members of the same club or association
become closely allied to one another, and able to act
together on occasions with unison and *esprit de corps ;*
and they will stand by one of their own number for
reasons precisely homologous to those which make a
member of one of the upper clubs support a fellow-mem-
ber if the latter happens to run for office. " He is a
gentleman, and shall have my vote," says the swell club
man. " He's one of the boys, and I'm for him," replies
the heeler from the district party association. In each
case the feeling is social rather than political, but where
the club man influences one vote the heeler controls ten.
A rich merchant and a small tradesman alike find it
merely a bore to attend the meetings of the local political club ; it is to them an irksome duty which is shirked

whenever possible. But to the small politicians and to the various workers and hangers-on, these meetings have a distinct social attraction, and attendance is a matter of preference. They are in congenial society and in the place where by choice they spend their evenings, and where they bring their friends and associates ; and naturally all the men so brought together gradually blend their social and political ties, and work with an effectiveness impossible to the outside citizens whose social instincts interfere, instead of coinciding, with their political duties. If an ordinary citizen wishes to have a game of cards or a talk with some of his companions, he must keep away from the local headquarters of his party ; whereas, under similar circumstances, the professional politician must go there. The man who is fond of his home naturally prefers to stay there in the evenings, rather than go out among the noisy club *habitués*, whose pleasure it is to see each other at least weekly, and who spend their evenings discussing neither sport, business, nor scandal, as do other sections of the community, but the equally monotonous subject of ward politics.

The strength of our political organizations arises from their development as social bodies ; many of the hardest workers in their ranks are neither office-holders nor yet paid henchmen, but merely members who have gradually learned to identify their fortunes with the party whose hall they have come to regard as the headquarters in which to spend the most agreeable of their leisure moments. Under the American system it is impossible for a man to accomplish anything by himself ;

he must associate himself with others, and they must throw their weight together. This is just what the social functions of the political clubs enable their members to do. The great and rich society clubs are composed of men who are not apt to take much interest in politics anyhow, and never act as a body. The immense effect produced by a social organization for political purposes is shown by the career of the Union League Club; and equally striking proof can be seen by every man who attends a ward meeting. There is thus, however much to be regretted it may be, a constant tendency towards the concentration of political power in the hands of those men who by taste and education are fitted to enjoy the social side of the various political organizations.

THE LIQUOR-SELLER IN POLITICS.

IT is this that gives the liquor-sellers their enormous influence in politics. Preparatory to the general election of 1884, there were held in the various districts of New York ten hundred and seven primaries and political conventions of all parties, and of these no less than six hundred and thirty-three took place in liquor-saloons,— a showing that leaves small ground for wonder at the low average grade of the nominees. The reason for such a condition of things is perfectly evident; it is because the liquor-saloons are places of social resort for the same men who turn the local political organizations into social clubs. Bar-tenders form perhaps the nearest approach to a leisure class that we have at present on this side of the water. They naturally are on semi-inti-

mate terms with all who frequent their houses. There
is no place where more gossip is talked than in bar-
rooms, and much of this gossip is about politics,—that
is, the politics of the ward, not of the nation. The
tariff and the silver question may be alluded to and civil
service reform may be incidentally damned, but the real
interest comes in discussing the doings of the men with
whom they are personally acquainted : why Billy so-
and-so, the alderman, has quarrelled with his former
chief supporter; whether " old man X " has really managed to fix the delegates to a given convention ; the
reason why one faction bolted at the last primary ; and
if it is true that a great down-town boss who has an
intimate friend of opposite political faith running in an
up-town district has forced the managers of his own
party to put up a man of straw against him. The bar-
keeper is a man of much local power, and is, of course,
hail-fellow-well-met with his visitors, as he and they can
be of mutual assistance to one another. Even if of
different politics, their feelings towards each other are
influenced by personal considerations purely ; and,
indeed, this is true of most of the smaller bosses as
regards their dealings among themselves, for, as one of
them once remarked to me with enigmatic truthfulness,
"there are no politics in politics " of the lower sort—
which, being interpreted, means that a professional politician is much less apt to be swayed by the fact of a
man's being a Democrat or a Republican than he is by
his being a personal friend or foe. The liquor-saloons
thus become the social headquarters of the little knots
or cliques of men who take most interest in local politi-

cal affairs; and by an easy transition they become the political headquarters when the time for preparing for the elections arrives; and, of course, the good-will of the owners of the places is thereby propitiated,—an important point with men striving to control every vote possible.

The local political clubs also become to a certain extent mutual benefit associations. The men in them become pretty intimate with one another; and in the event of one becoming ill, or from any other cause thrown out of employment, his fellow-members will very often combine to assist him through his troubles, and quite large sums are frequently raised for such a purpose. Of course, this forms an additional bond among the members, who become closely knit together by ties of companionship, self-interest, and mutual interdependence. Very many members of these associations come into them without any thought of advancing their own fortunes; they work very hard for their party, or rather for the local body bearing the party name, but they do it quite disinterestedly, and from a feeling akin to that which we often see make other men devote their time and money to advancing the interests of a yacht club or racing stable, although no immediate benefit can result therefrom to themselves. One such man I now call to mind who is by no means well off, and is neither an office-seeker nor an office-holder, but who regularly every year spends about fifty dollars at election time for the success of the party, or rather the wing of the party, to which he belongs. He has a personal pride in seeing his pet candidates rolling up large majorities. Men of this

stamp also naturally feel most enthusiasm for, or ani-
mosity against, the minor candidates with whom they are
themselves acquainted. The names at the head of the
ticket do not, to their minds, stand out with much indi-
viduality ; and while such names usually command the
normal party support, yet very often there is an infinitely keener rivalry among the smaller politicians over
candidates for local offices. I remember, in 1880, a very
ardent Democratic ward club, many of the members of
which in the heat of a contest for an assembly-man
coolly swapped off quite a number of votes for President
in consideration of votes given to their candidate for the
State Legislature ; and in 1885, in my own district, a
local Republican club that had a member running for
alderman, performed a precisely similar feat in relation
to their party's candidate for Governor. A Tammany
State senator openly announced in a public speech that
it was of vastly more importance to Tammany to have
one of her own men Mayor of New York than it was to
have a Democratic President of the United States.
Very many of the leaders of the rival organizations, who
lack the boldness to make such a frankly cynical avowal
of what their party feeling really amounts to, yet in
practice, both as regards mayor and as regards all other
local offices which are politically or pecuniarily of importance, act exactly on the theory enunciated by the Tammany statesman ; and, as a consequence, in every great
election not only is it necessary to have the mass of the
voters waked up to the importance of the principles that
are at stake, but it also unfortunately is necessary to see
that the powerful local leaders are convinced that it will

be to their own interest to be faithful to the party ticket. Often there will be intense rivalry between two associations or two minor bosses; and one may take up and the other oppose the cause of a candidate with an earnestness and hearty good-will arising by no means from any feeling for the man himself, but from the desire to score a triumph over the opposition. It not unfrequently happens that a perfectly good man, who would not knowingly suffer the least impropriety in the conduct of his canvass, is supported in some one district by a little knot of politicians of shady character, who have nothing in common with him at all, but who wish to beat a rival body that is opposing him, and who do not for a moment hesitate to use every device, from bribery down, to accomplish their ends. A curious incident of this sort came to my knowledge while happening to inquire how a certain man became a Republican. It occurred a good many years ago, and thanks to our election laws it could not now be repeated in all its details; but affairs similar in kind occur at every election. I may preface it by stating that the man referred to, whom we will call X, ended by pushing himself up in the world, thanks to his own industry and integrity, and is now a well-to-do private citizen and as good a fellow as any one would wish to see. But at the time spoken of he was a young laborer, of Irish birth, working for his livelihood on the docks and associating with his Irish and American fellows. The district where he lived was overwhelmingly Democratic, and the contests were generally merely factional. One small politician, a saloon-keeper named Larry, who had a good deal of influence, used to enlist on election day, by pay and other compensation, the services of the gang of young fellows to which X belonged. On one occasion he failed to reward them for their work, and in other ways treated them so shabbily as to make them very angry, more especially X, who was their leader. There was no way to pay him off until the next election; but they determined to break his influence utterly then, and as the best method for doing this they decided to "vote as far away from him" as possible, or, in other words, to strain every nerve to secure the election of all the candidates most opposed to those whom Larry favored. After due consultation, it was thought that this could be most surely done by supporting the Republican ticket. Most of the other bodies of young laborers, or, indeed, of young roughs, made common cause with X and his friends. Everything was kept very quiet until election day, neither Larry nor the few Republicans having an inkling of what was going on. It was a rough district, and usually the Republican booths were broken up and their ballot-distributors driven off early in the day; but on this occasion, to the speechless astonishment of everybody, things went just the other way. The Republican ballots were distributed most actively, the opposing workers were bribed, persuaded, or frightened away, all means fair and foul were tried, and finally there was almost a riot,—the outcome being that the Republicans actually obtained a majority in a district where they had never before polled ten per cent. of the total vote. Such a phenomenon attracted the attention of the big Republican leaders, who after some inquiry found it was due to X. To show their gratitude and to secure so useful an ally permanently (for this was before the days of civil-service reform), they procured him a lucrative place in the New York Post-office; and he, in turn, being a man of natural parts, at once seized the opportunity, set to work to correct the defects of his early education, and is now what I have described him to be.

BOSS METHODS.

A POLITICIAN who becomes an influential local leader or boss is, of course, always one with a genuine talent for intrigue and organization. He owes much of his power to the rewards he is able to dispense. Not only does he procure for his supporters positions in the service of the state or city,—as in the custom-house, sheriff's office, etc.,—but he is also able to procure positions for many on horse railroads, the elevated roads, quarry works, etc. Great corporations are peculiarly subject to the attacks of demagogues, and they find it greatly to their interest to be on good terms with the leader in each district who controls the vote of the assemblyman and alderman; and therefore the former is pretty sure that a letter of recommendation from him on behalf of any applicant for work will receive most favorable consideration. The leader also is continually helping his henchmen out of difficulties, pecuniary and otherwise; he lends them a dollar or two now and then, helps out, when possible, such of their kinsmen as get into the clutches of the law, gets a hold over such of them as have done wrong and are afraid of being exposed, and learns to judiciously mix bullying with the rendering of service.

But in addition to all this, the boss owes very much of his commanding influence to his social relations with various bodies of his constituents; and it is his work as well as his pleasure to keep these relations up. No *débutante* during her first winter in society has a more exacting round of social duties to perform than has a prominent ward politician. In every ward there are numerous organizations, primarily social in character, but capable of being turned to good account politically. The Amalgamated Hack-drivers' Union, the Hibernian Republican Club, the West Side Young Democrats, the Jefferson C. Mullin Picnic Association,—there are twenty such bodies as these in every district, and with, at any rate, the master spirits in each and all it is necessary for the boss to keep on terms of intimate and, indeed, rather boisterous friendship. When the Jefferson C. Mullin society goes on a picnic, the average citizen scrupulously avoids its neighborhood ; but the boss goes, perhaps with his wife, and, moreover, enjoys himself heartily, and is hail-fellow-well-met with the rest of the picnickers, who, by the way, may be by no means bad fellows ; and when election day comes round, the latter, in return, no matter to what party they may nominally belong, enthusiastically support their friend and guest on social, not political, grounds. The boss knows every man in his district who can control any number of votes : an influential saloon-keeper, the owner of a large livery stable, the leader among a set of horse-car drivers, a foreman in a machine-shop who has a taste for politics,—with all alike he keeps up constant and friendly relations. Of course this fact does not of itself make the boss a bad man ; there are several such I could point out who are ten times over better fellows than are the mild-mannered scholars of timorous virtue who criticise them. But on the whole the qualities tending to make a man a successful local political leader under our present conditions are not apt to be qualities that make him serve the public honestly or disinterestedly ; and in the lower wards, where there is a large vicious population, the condition of politics is often fairly appalling, and the boss of the dominant party is generally a man of grossly immoral public and private character, as any one can satisfy himself by examining the testimony taken by the last two or three legislative committees that have investigated the affairs of New York city. In some of these wards many of the social organizations with which the leaders are obliged to keep on good terms are composed of criminals, or of the relatives and associates of criminals. The testimony mentioned above showed some strange things. I will take at random a few instances that occur to me at the moment. There was one case of an assemblyman who served several terms in the Legislature, while his private business was to carry on corrupt negotiations between the excise commissioners and owners of low haunts who wished licenses. The president of a powerful semi-political association was by profession a burglar ; the man who received the goods he stole was an alderman. Another alderman was elected while his hair was still short from a term in State prison. A school trustee had been convicted of embezzlement, and was the associate of criminals. A prominent official in the police department was interested in disreputable houses and gambling-saloons, and was backed politically by their proprietors.

BEATING THE MACHINE.

IN the better wards the difficulty comes in drilling a little sense and energy into decent people; they either do not care to combine or else refuse to learn how. In one district we did at one time and for a considerable period get control of affairs and elect a set of almost ideal delegates and candidates to the various nominating and legislative bodies, and in the end took an absolutely commanding although temporary position in State and even in national politics.

This was done by the efforts of some twenty or thirty young fellows who devoted a large part of their time thoroughly to organizing and getting out the respectable vote. The moving spirits were all active, energetic men, with common sense, whose motives were perfectly disinterested. Some went in from principle; others, doubtless, from good-fellowship or sheer love of the excitement always attendant upon a political struggle. Our success was due to our absolute freedom from caste spirit. Among our chief workers were a Columbia College professor, a crack oarsman from the same institution, an Irish quarryman, a master carpenter, a rich young merchant, the owner of a small cigar store, the editor of a little German newspaper, and a couple of employees from the post-office and custom-house, who worked directly against their own seeming interests. One of our important committees was composed of a prominent member of a Jewish synagogue, of the son of a noted Presbyterian clergyman, and of a young Catholic lawyer. We won some quite remarkable triumphs, for the first time in New York politics, carrying primaries against the machine, and as the result of our most successful struggle completely revolutionizing the State convention held to send delegates to the National Republican Convention of 1884, and returning to that body, for the first and only time it was ever done, a solid delegation of Independent Republicans. This was done, however, by sheer hard work on the part of a score or so of men ; the mass of our good citizens, even after the victories which they had assisted in winning, understood nothing about how they were won. Many of them actually objected to organizing, apparently having a confused idea that we could always win by what one of their number called a "spontaneous uprising," to which a quiet young fellow in our camp grimly responded that he had done a good deal of political work in his day, but that he never in his life had worked so hard and so long as he did to get up the "spontaneous" movement in which we were then engaged.

CONCLUSIONS.

IN conclusion, it may be accepted as a fact, however unpleasant, that if steady work and much attention to detail are required, ordinary citizens, to whom participation in politics is merely a disagreeable duty, will always be beaten by the organized army of politicians to whom it is both duty, business, and pleasure, and who are knit together and to outsiders by their social relations. On the other hand, average citizens do take a spasmodic interest in public affairs ; and we should therefore so shape our governmental system that the action required by the voters should be as simple and direct as possible, and should not need to be taken any more often than is necessary. Governmental power should be concentrated in the hands of a very few men, who would be so conspicuous that no citizen could help knowing all about them; and the elections should not come too frequently. Not one decent voter in ten will take the trouble annually to inform himself as to the character of the host of petty candidates to be balloted for, but he will be sure to know all about the mayor, comptroller, etc. It is not to his credit that we can only rely, and that without much certainty, upon his taking a spasmodic interest in the government that affects his own well-being; but such is the case, and accordingly we ought, as far as possible, to have a system requiring on his part intermittent and not sustained action.   *Theodore Roosevelt.*

www.ingramcontent.com/pod-product-compliance
Lightning Source LLC
Chambersburg PA
CBHW021525270326
41930CB00008B/1103